MY
AFRICAN
ME TOO

Dedication

We dedicate this book to all of our beautiful children and grandchildren.

We love you so very much!

We would also like to acknowledge all of the beautiful African children of the world. We hope that you are loving yourselves as much as we are loving you.

Note to Parents....

Our prayer is that you will allow this book to be a foundational teaching for you and your children. It is so important that you know who you are and how great you are; but it is even more important that we make sure every African child knows too.

INTRODUCTION

Did you know that all of your *Talents*, *Abilities*, and *Beauty* come from inside of you? The goodness in your *Heart* and *Soul* is what makes you good, and that causes you to do the things that benefit the world. These *Inner Qualities* are in you from the time you are born, and will Increase when you *Nurture* them, as you grow older.

As a *baby* you were Good, no trouble at all. You really couldn't talk, but you blessed so many people. Your smile made other people smile, Your laugh made everyone laugh. Your giggle tickled everyone's Soul, and you were the Joy of Your Family's life.

As a *toddler* you begin to crawl, and away you would go. You started standing and sitting, and even moving slow. One step, two step, three, and four; you went from being in one place to moving through doors. Up and down steps, indoors and out, now as a toddler you have movement, all throughout the house.

Your arms will become strong and your feet will become quick. You can dance and sing, read, count and fix.

You will grow real fast by eating good foods!

Your *vegetables* will make you stronger than you ever thought they would. You will become taller, and over things you will be able to see. You will also be able to reach and grab new kinds of stuff. Running, jumping and playing will be easier; new games will be fun to learn and do.

Look at your eyes, your nose, your lips, they tell you about your family's history and where you come from. There is a good feeling inside of You, it says "You are welcomed".

We have our African *Ancestors* to thank for such beautiful gifts and qualities that we can *achieve*. These gifts of qualities are the *foundation* of people being their Best. They help us live in Love, *Peace*, and *Harmony*.

All of this says that you are *African*, a place of sunlight and animals, a beautiful land. *Africa* is the place where everything begins. Where trees become trees and wind becomes wind.

Pangaea was the Earth, it was one complete land. But then it split apart and our portion is African.

BEFORE

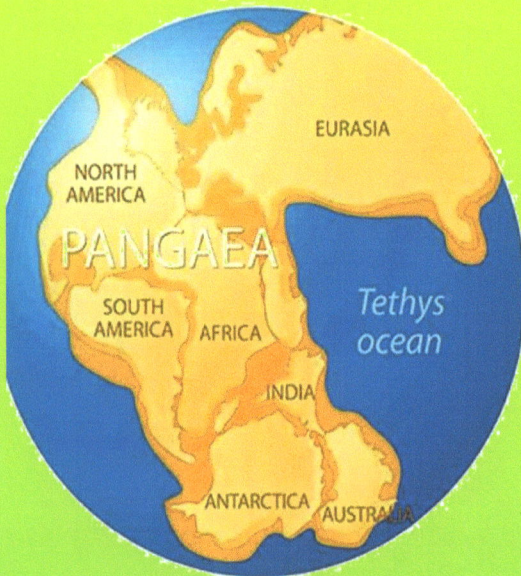

AFTER

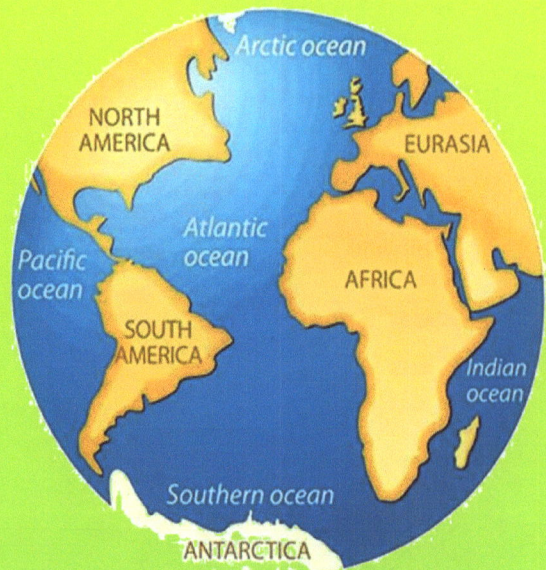

Do you want to know something very special? There is a place that everyone and everything can be *traced* back to; and that place is called Africa. There are other names that Africa has been called; like *Ethiopia*, *Kemet*, and *Alkebu-lan*. Africa's many names come from the different ways that people knew of it. Some people knew about Africa's waters, many knew about the animals, some knew about the people, and others knew about the land.

You are African, that is the name of our land. It was also called *Kemet*, **Alkebu-lan** and *Ethiopian*. *Ethiopia* means that the sun has touched you. That it has kissed your skin to a wonderful hue.

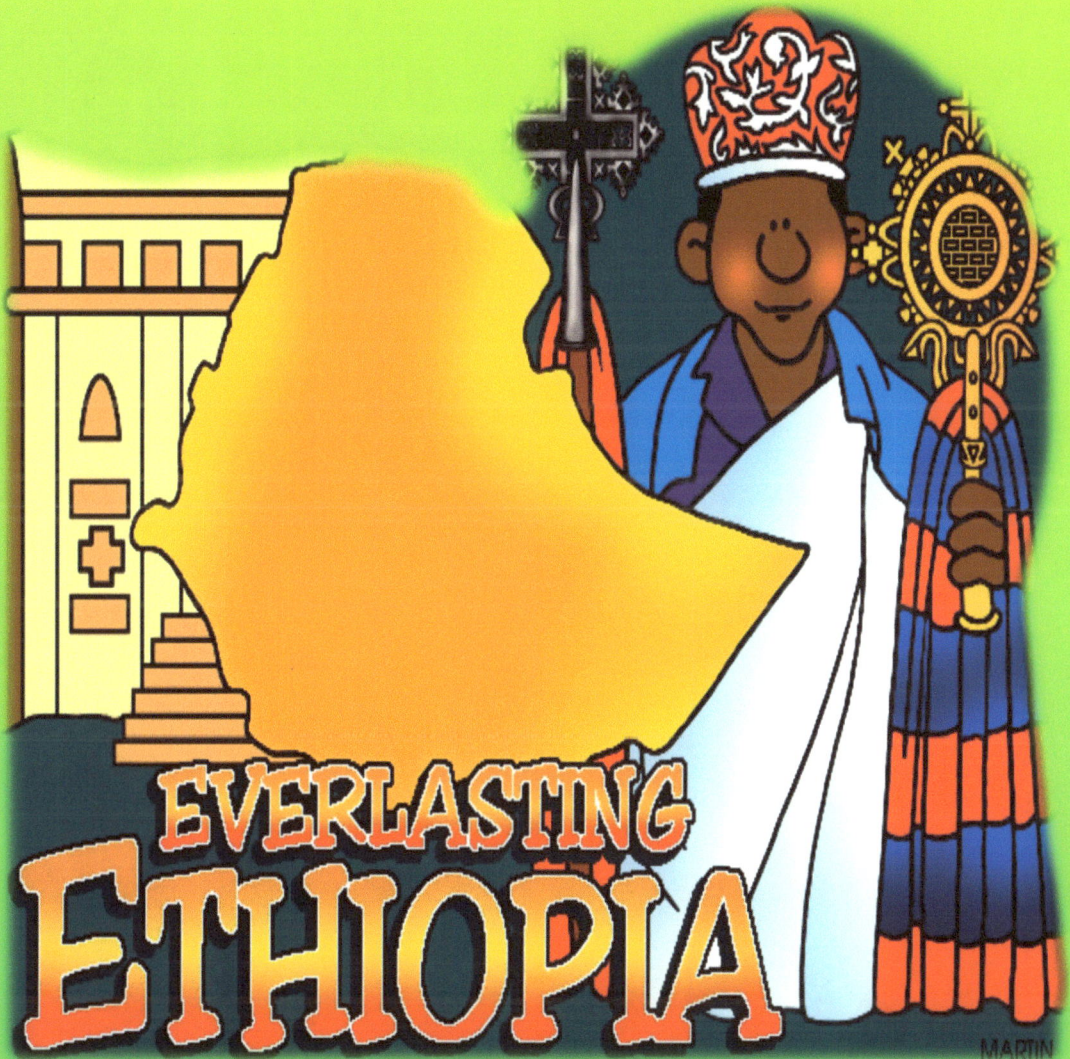

EVERLASTING ETHIOPIA

MARTIN

There is something inside of You called *Deoxyribonucleic Acid* or *D.N.A*... It is the reason you are living today. *D.N.A* tells your body how it should look. *African* *D.N.A.,* is the oldest in the book.

Your color of skin is from *melanin*. It is all over you from top to end. A gift that is Great, a beautiful prize, you get light and dark colors, light and dark eyes.

You are a *Human Descent* of the *Continent* now known as Africa. It does not matter what is seen in the mirror. The Origin of man and woman, the people that we see all around us, is Africa.

African Languages Matters

From Africa, we have all of our different *Races*, *Cultures*, *Societies*, and *Religions.* As our *population* grew, our ancestors *migrated* and lived in the other lands. Those other lands allowed our ancestors to be different and do different things like: *languages*, *education*, dressing, foods, cooking, playing, and celebrating. All of that makes the world special. All of it can be Traced back to Africa.

Living in these new areas with colder *temperatures* and *higher altitudes* caused our bodies to make changes, Our skin got lighter so that we could make more *Vitamin D*. Our hair changed *texture* to protect our head and necks. Our eyes and noses adapted to the light, wind and cold, so that we could see and breathe better. Even our hands and feet adapted to the different *terrestrial* *conditions* that we were now exposed to. We changed a little on the outside. We started to look like different people. But we never changed on the inside. We are still the same.

Social Order/Laws

AFRICA

Once we were able to stay in one place for long periods of time, because we could now grow food and raise animals, we *created* rules so that everyone could get along. We *taught* how to treat each other, and we *learned* how to *judge* what was *right* and what was *wrong*. The *Elders*, who had lived the longest, helped show everyone what was *justice* and *equality*. Sometimes they would even tell us what we would grow up to be, and that helped us know our own abilities.

TRADE/ECONOMY

Once our different groups got *settled* and understood the areas, we would give them some of the food, animals, and stuff that we had for some of their food, animals, and stuff. We used to *barter* to make *deals*. That means that I would give you something good, like fish, and you would give me something good, like fruits. We didn't have money yet. This was the best way to *trade*. Eventually we started using *stones*, *sea shells*, special *rocks*, special *tree leaves*, and other things to *pay* for the things that we wanted.

Agriculture

Our Ancestors begin to establish *communities* all over the world. They were *hunters* and *gatherers* first. Then they begin to learn how some of the foods they liked grew from *plants* and *trees*. They learned how to *plant seeds* and watch their *crops* grow. Eventually *farming* became their way of life, and they loved it. From farming they learned to raise *cattle*, *sheep*, and different *birds* to eat. Now they could spend a lot of time *observing*, *thinking*, *studying* and *learning* things that were around them.

BELIEFS

Sometimes we were in places that looked so different to us. As we thought about these places we knew that God must have made it just for us to live. So we always made sure that we *worshipped* God in those areas, and we used the things that he gave us, in those areas, to show that we were *praising* him. We had *rituals*, we *painted* on cave walls, we *stacked rocks*, and we *carved rocks* too. We made *songs* and *stories* describing God in these new places that we discovered Him in.

Africa gave rise to God, Queens, and Kings, and spoke to the world the start of these Beings. Africa says and mentions that angels exist too, not just in books and art but inside you. In Africa, God's *melanin* is inside, not skin, but we wear it as a covering to remember our kin.

I WANT TO GROW UP AND BE...

It is time for you to think about yourself, and what it is that you want to be. Look into the mirror and see. Are these _doctor_ eyes, a _teachers_ nose, or a speakers lips? Do you want to help others, or birds, or trees? Do you want to fly _planes_ or be captain of _ships_? It is you who can dream, you who can wish. Just look into the _mirror_ and give yourself that gift.

Once you decide, think about two more, or three. You don't have to just be one thing, you can be all that you want to be.

All it takes is study and _preparation_, _effort_ and hard work. You can do it. Yes you can. Do more, do better, be the best that you can.

GLOSSARY

Africa [af-ri-kuh] **:** Continents South of Europe and between the Atlantic and Indian Oceans.

African [af-ri-kuh n] **:** of or relating to Africa or people of African descent.

Ancestors [af-ri-kuh n] **:** a person, typically one more remote than a grandparent, from whom one is descended.

Alkebu-lan [al ke bu lan]: The ancient name of Africa

Baby [bey-bee] **:** a very young child, especially one newly or recently born.

Barter [bahr-ter] **:** exchange (goods or services) for other goods or services without using money.

Beauty [byoo-tee] **:** a combination of qualities, such as shape, color, or form, that pleases the aesthetic senses, especially the sight.

Bird [burd]: a warm-blooded egg-laying vertebrate distinguished by the possession of feathers, wings, and a beak and (typically) by being able to fly.

Cattle[kat-l]: large ruminant animals with horns and cloven hoofs, domesticated for meat or milk, or as beasts of burden; cows.

Communities [kuh-myoo-ni-tees] **:** a group of people living in the same place or having a particular characteristic in common.

Continent [kon-tn-uh nt] **:** any of the world's main continuous expanses of land (Africa, Antarctica, Asia, Australia, Europe, North America, South America).

Created [kree-eyt] **:** bring (something) into existence.

Crops [krops] **:** a cultivated plant that is grown as food, especially a grain, fruit, or vegetable.

Cultures [kuhl-chers] **:** the arts and other manifestations of human intellectual achievement regarded collectively.

Deals [deels] : an agreement entered into by two or more parties for their mutual benefit, especially in a business or political context.

Deoxyribonucleic acid (D.N.A.) [dee-ok-si-rahy-boh-noo-klee-ik, -nyoo -, -ok-si-rahy-] : the fundamental and distinctive characteristics or qualities of someone or something, especially when regarded as unchangeable.

Doctor [dok-ters] : a qualified practitioner of medicine; a physician.

Education [ej-oo-key-shuh n] : the process of receiving or giving systematic instruction, especially at a school or university.

Elders [el-ders] : of one or more out of a group of related or otherwise associated people of a greater age.

Ethiopia [ee-thee-oh-pee-uh] : an ancient region in NE Africa, bordering on Egypt and the Red Sea.

Ethiopian [ee-thee-oh-pee-uh n] : a native or inhabitant of Ethiopia, or a person of Ethiopian descent.

Equality [ih-kwol-i-tee] : the state of being equal, especially in status, rights, and opportunities.

Farming [fahr-ming] : the activity or business of growing crops and raising livestock.

Gatherers [gath -er er s] : an assembly or meeting, especially a social or festive one or one held for a specific purpose.

Harmony [hahr-muh-nee] : the combination of simultaneously sounded musical notes to produce chords and chord progressions having a pleasing effect.

Heart [hahrt] : the central or innermost part of something.

Higher altitude [hahy al-ti-tood, -tyood] : the height of an object or point in relation to sea level or ground level.

Human Descent [hyoo-muh n ,dee-suh nt] : a person deriving from an ancestor; lineage; extraction.

Hunter [huhn-ter] : a person or animal that hunts.

Inner Qualities [in-er kwol-i-tees] : of honesty, courage, or the like; integrity: It takes character to face up to a bully.

Judge [juhj] : form an opinion or conclusion about.

Kemet [kim et] : the name for Ancient Egypt. It means: "black land", because of the fertile black soils of the Nile flood plains.

Languages [lang-gwij] : the method of human communication, either spoken or written, consisting of the use of words in a structured and conventional way.

Learned [lurn d] : (of a person) having much knowledge acquired by study.

Learning [lurn ing] : knowledge acquired through experience, study, or being taught.

Leaves [leevz] : a thing that resembles a leaf in being flat and thin, typically something that is one of two or more similar items forming a set or stack.

Melanin [mel-uh-nin] : a dark brown to black pigment occurring in the hair, skin, and iris of the eye in people and animals. It is responsible for tanning of skin exposed to sunlight.

Mirror [mir-er] : a reflective surface, now typically of glass coated with a metal amalgam, that reflects a clear image.

Observing [uh b-zurv ing] : notice or perceive (something) and register it as being significant.

Painted [peyn-tid] : cover the surface of (something) with paint, as decoration or protection.

Pay [pey] : give (someone) money that is due for work done, goods received, or a debt incurred.

Pangaea [pan-jee-uh] : is a hypothetical supercontinent that included all current land masses, believed to have been in existence before the continents broke apart during the Triassic and Jurassic Periods.

Peace [pees] : freedom from disturbance; quiet and tranquility.

Planes [pleyns] : A heavier-than-air aircraft kept aloft by the upward thrust exerted by the passing air on its fixed wings and driven by propellers, jet propulsion, etc.

Plants [plahnt] : a living organism of the kind exemplified by trees, shrubs, herbs, grasses, ferns, and mosses, typically growing in a permanent site, absorbing water and inorganic substances through its roots, and synthesizing nutrients in its leaves by photosynthesis using the green pigment chlorophyll.

Plant seeds [plahnt seeds] : a small object produced by a *plant* from which a new *plant* can grow

Praising [preyz] : express one's respect and gratitude toward (a deity), especially in song.

Preparation [prep-uh-rey-shuh n] : the action or process of making ready or being made ready for use or consideration.

Race [reys] : A contest of speed, as in running, riding, driving, or sailing.

Right [rahyt] : morally good, justified, or acceptable.

Rituals [rich-oo-uh ls] : a series of actions or type of behavior regularly and invariably followed by someone.

Rocks [roks] : the solid mineral material forming part of the surface of the earth and other similar planets, exposed on the surface or underlying the soil or oceans.

Sea [see] : the expanse of salt water that covers most of the earth's surface and surrounds its landmasses.

Settled [set-l d] : adopt a more steady or secure style of life, especially in a permanent job and home.

Soul [sohl] : the spiritual or immaterial part of a human being or animal, regarded as immortal.

Sheep [sheep] : a domesticated ruminant animal with a thick woolly coat and (typically only in the male) curving horns.

Shells [shels] : the hard protective outer case of a mollusk or crustacean.

Ships [ships] : a vessel larger than a boat for transporting people or goods by sea.

Societies [suh-sahy-i-tees] : the community of people living in a particular country or region and having shared customs, laws, and organizations.

Songs [sawng] : a short poem or other set of words set to music or meant to be sung.

Stones [stohns] : the hard, solid, nonmetallic mineral matter of which rock is made, especially as a building material.

Stories [stohr-ees] : an account of past events in someone's life or in the evolution of something.

Studying [stuhd-ee-ing] : devote time and attention to acquiring knowledge on (an academic subject), especially by means of books.

Talents [tal-uh nt] : natural aptitude or skill.

Taught [tawt] : show or explain to (someone) how to do something.

Teacher [tee-cher] : a person who teaches, especially in a school.

Temperatures [tem-per-uh-chers] : the degree or intensity of heat present in a substance or object, especially as expressed according to a comparative scale and shown by a thermometer or perceived by touch.

Terrestrial [tuh-res-tree-uh l] : of, on, or relating to the earth.

Texture [teks-cher] : the feel, appearance, or consistency of a surface or a substance.

Thinking [thing-king] : the process of using one's mind to consider or reason about something.

Toddler [tod-ler] : a young child who is just beginning to walk.

Traced [treys d] : find or discover by investigation.

Trade [treyd] : exchange (something) for something else, typically as a commercial transaction.

Trees [trees] : a woody perennial plant, typically having a single stem or trunk growing to a considerable height and bearing lateral branches at some distance from the ground.

Vegetables [vej-tuh-buh l s] : a plant or part of a plant used as food, typically as accompaniment to meat or fish, such as a cabbage, potato, carrot, or bean.

Worshipped [wur-ship d] : show reverence and adoration for (a deity); honor with religious rites.

Wrong [rong] : not correct or true. unjust, dishonest, or immoral.

THaNK YoU!

IF YOU ARE INTERESTED IN WRITING AND PUBLISHING WITH SOLOMON & MAKEDA PUBLISHING, VISIT US AT WWW.SM4PUBLISHING.COM TODAY

www.ingramcontent.com/pod-product-compliance
Lightning Source LLC
Chambersburg PA
CBHW041553040426
42447CB00002B/176